D0482346

SISU

FIND YOUR RESILIENCE
THE FINNISH WAY
SISU

JUSTYN BARNES

STERLING ETHOS
New York

STERLING ETHOS
New York

An Imprint of Sterling Publishing Co., Inc.
1166 Avenue of the Americas
New York, NY 10036

STERLING ETHOS and the distinctive Sterling Ethos logo
are registered trademarks of Sterling Publishing Co., Inc.

© 2020 Quarto Publishing PLC,
an imprint of The Quarto Group

All rights reserved. No part of this publication may be
reproduced, stored in a retrieval system, or transmitted
in any form or by any means (including electronic,
mechanical, photocopying, recording, or otherwise)
without prior written permission from the publisher.

ISBN 978-1-4549-3919-1

Distributed in Canada by Sterling Publishing Co., Inc.,
c/o Canadian Manda Group,
664 Annette Street, Toronto, Ontario
M6S 2C8, Canada

For information about custom editions, special sales,
and premium and corporate purchases, please contact
Sterling Special Sales at 800-805-5489
or specialsales@sterlingpublishing.com.

Manufactured in Singapore

10 9 8 7 6 5 4 3 2 1

sterlingpublishing.com

For picture credits, see page 160

MIX
Paper from
responsible sources
FSC® C016973

CONTENTS

INTRODUCTION

We all encounter seemingly insurmountable problems at times. In such situations, have you ever surprised yourself with your levels of fortitude and perseverance and your ability to push through and triumph over adversity? If so, you may have unwittingly tapped into an inner power that people in Finland call *sisu* (pronounced SEE-soo).

It is a word that defies simple translation, but with a constructive sisu mind-set, problems are confronted courageously, challenges are reframed as opportunities for growth, setbacks are perceived as blips, and solutions are pursued with tenacity and creativity.

Sisu engenders a gritty, can-do spirit where purpose leads to action and surrendering tamely when the going gets tough doesn't cross your mind. And by nurturing it in our daily lives, we can become more resilient, better problem-solvers, and what once might have seemed highly improbable becomes feasible.

Sisu has been a cornerstone of Finnish culture for more than 500 years, underpinning its survival and catalyzing the miraculous transformation of independent Finland from a poor country into one of the world's most prosperous nations on almost every indicator of well-being. By giving it a name and making it a guiding ethos, the Finns have been better able to access their sisu and reap the benefits. But sisu is within us all, and I hope that this book will help you to understand and unleash its amazing potential. Applied with honesty, integrity, kindness, and consideration for others, sisu can be positively life changing.

Justyn Barnes

1

ROOTS
OF SISU

Let's begin by exploring some of the
ways in which the Finnish people's sense
of sisu has influenced the development
of their country and culture.

LATENT STRENGTH

———

The meanings attributed to the word *sisu* have evolved over the centuries. It derives from the Finnish *sisus*, which refers to guts or the interior of an object. The first written instances of sisu occurred in the 1500s, when it was used to describe a personal characteristic or natural tendency. The related word *sisucunda* was defined in an eighteenth-century Finnish dictionary as the place in the human body where strong emotions originate. In recent times, researchers have suggested it's more a matter of mind-set than gutsiness. What is beyond dispute is that sisu is a potent force within that can help people exceed their known capabilities.

Winter Warriors

———

The 1939–40 Winter War that followed the Soviet Union's invasion of Finland drew international attention to the strength of Finnish sisu. Despite being outnumbered by at least three to one and having considerably less firepower— the Red Army had one hundred times more tanks and thirty times as many aircrafts—the Finns managed to fend off their belligerent neighbor. "Finnish phantoms," so-called because they wore a white outer layer as camouflage in the snow, executed their strategy better than the Soviets in temperatures as low as –49°F (–45°C). This unlikely success was underpinned by the Finns' indomitable spirit.

66 The Finns have something they call *sisu*. It is a compound of bravado and bravery, of ferocity and tenacity, of the ability to keep fighting after most people would have quit, and to fight with the will to win. 99

———

The New York Times, January 14, 1940

Sauna and Self-care

———

The sauna is a Finnish invention dating back thousands of years. It evolved from a tent-like structure to a pit in the ground to a log cabin, and today there are 3.3 million saunas for Finland's population of 5.5 million. Its significance is such that past generations often erected a sauna before building the family home, and it was used for childbirth as well as preparing the deceased for burial. Just as the evaporating hot steam (*löyly*) reinvigorated crofters of yore to persevere through brutal winters, the sauna remains a place where Finns regularly go to recharge physically, mentally, and spiritually. Such self-care is key to cultivating sisu.

Poetry from the Soul

In the spring of 1828, Elias Lönnrot began
the huge undertaking of collecting folk songs and
poetry from all over Finland. It took him fifteen years
and eleven field trips to do it. The vision and perseverance
required to complete his mission was an act of sisu in itself.
And the ultimate result was the *Kalevala*, an extraordinary
compilation of 27,795 verses divided into fifty folk stories
to create a national epic. It was the first time many
of the poems—often performed as songs over the
centuries—had been written down. Capturing the soul
of Finland, the *Kalevala* galvanized its people's pride
and push for independence. It endures today as
a central symbol of the rich Finnish culture.

NEW FRONTIERS

—

Sisu can help you to adapt and survive periods
of extreme upheaval. This was apparent during the
"Great Migration" of Finnish people to North America
between 1870 and 1930. The Finns labored in mines,
farms, forests, and factories, gaining a reputation as
doggedly hard workers. Quick to save up and purchase plots
of land of their own, they were also admired for their thrift.
They organized their own labor movements and led strikes
for improved working conditions, persisting against the
might of corporations who demonized them as "Commies"
for doing what was right and fair. They built tight-knit
communities and helped each other through lean periods.
No matter what needed to be done, the Finns stepped up.

Debts Repaid

After World War I, Finland had debts to pay.
The difference between its response and that of some
wealthier countries in the same position is that Finland took
systematic action to repay their loans as soon as possible.
Americans were full of respect and praise for the Finns
when they were paid back in full in 1933.
Again, after signing a mutual assistance agreement with
Russia following World War II, Finland reimbursed its
erstwhile rulers within ten years. Perhaps this aversion to
being indebted reflects a desire to remain free and self-
reliant after centuries under foreign rule. The qualities of
integrity, reliability, and honesty associated with Finnish
sisu demanded they made sacrifices to do what was needed.
A promise is a promise that must be kept.

Doing the Impossible

———

To get a feel for the historical struggles of the Finnish people, listen to composer Jean Sibelius's symphonic tone poem *Finlandia*. Sibelius wrote the first version in 1899, and it became an unofficial national anthem at a time when the Grand Duchy of Finland was under the thumb of the Russian Empire. To evade Russian censorship, it had to be performed under various less provocative names (such as "Happy Feelings at the Awakening of Finnish Spring"), but Sibelius's intent was unmistakable. The rumbling, tempestuous music stirred the patriotic pride of Finns to persevere in their quest for independence. "Sisu is like a metaphorical shot in the arm that allows the individual to do what's impossible," said Sibelius, and his enduringly popular work *Finlandia* is a testament to that spirit.

GET HAPPY

The 2019 United Nations World Happiness Report ranked Finland at number one for the second year running. What is the country's secret? Why don't those notoriously high tax bills get the Finns down? Well, perhaps it's because those taxes are invested in an education system that offers equal opportunities for all, and social support systems that will break citizens' fall when they are at their weakest. And maybe sisu has helped too, giving Finnish people the drive to tackle the essential issues affecting their society first, on the understanding that doing so creates a strong foundation to then focus on, and pursue, personal goals. Happiness is a place between too little and too much, as the Finnish saying goes, so always prioritize well-being over wealth.

Sisu Emoji

As befits such a pioneering country, Finland was the
first to create its own set of country-specific emojis.
The collection of fifty-six emojis celebrates some legendary
Finns and visually articulates some uniquely Finnish
customs, words, and emotions—from the singular joy
of defeating their neighbor Sweden at sport to a craving
for the salty licorice sweet *salmiakki*. Naturally, a sisu
emoji is included. It features a person punching out of
a rock, inspired by the Finnish proverb *Luja tahto vie läpi
harmaan kiven* ("a strong will leads you through the gray
stone"). So, if you ever feel as if your path ahead is blocked
by a wall, think of the sisu emoji and smash through it!

2

FIND YOUR
RESILIENCE

Times of tribulation invite us to dig deep
into our reserves of sisu to find an extra gear,
take action, and bounce back.

Embrace Adversity

———

Life is punctuated by major challenges.
But once you learn how to access your personal sisu,
you can greet any severe misfortune like an old friend.
Give it a hug, have a convivial chat, and find out what's
going on. Reflect on times past when you may have had to
deal with similar situations. And when you get to the root
of the problem, take action. Then it's time to bid a fond
farewell, knowing that next time adversity pays a visit,
you will be a little bit stronger, more self-aware,
and better equipped to deal with it.

> **"** Sisu is a Finnish word and way of life. Sisu is the courage, strength, and perserverance to conquer tragedy and rise above any and all adversity. **"**

———

Marko Albrecht, filmmaker

Spring Will Come

———

The harshness of the Finnish climate is a key historical factor underpinning sisu. Each year, eight long months of winter entomb the landscape in frost, and nothing grows. But over the centuries, Finns who work the land have found ways to be resourceful and resilient, developing methods to survive through these dark, barren days. They know that, if they can endure such privations and do not yield, the ice will eventually melt and green shoots will emerge. Even in the most taxing times, know that, if you draw on your inner sisu, spring will always come.

"Fools" Prosper

Before becoming Finland's first head of government,
Oskari Tokoi spent long hours laboring in the mines
of Wyoming and Colorado during the 1890s. In his
autobiography, *Sisu: Even Through a Stone Wall*, Tokoi
relates the story of how he and a workmate cheated death
after a mining accident, first by crawling in a two-foot
(60 cm) layer of clean air under a poisonous cloud and then
running through intense heat to a safe spot 100 feet (30 m)
higher up. They overheard someone in the rescue squad say:
"Those damned fools must be dead." "We damned fools
aren't dead," Tokoi shouted back. "We're here! We're
alright!" And once the corridor was clear of poisonous gas,
Tokoi and his companion quietly went back to work.

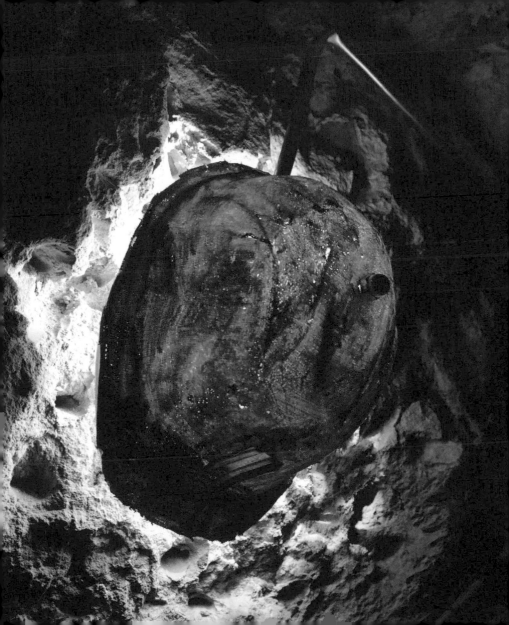

Educated Optimism

—

While sisu is grounded in a realistic attitude,
it also requires a streak of optimism. Finns are not
known to be overtly optimistic types, but nevertheless
they have it. Not the kind of blind optimism that has no
basis in fact, but a deep-seated belief based on real-world
experience that things can and will get better no matter
how bleak the current situation. This outlook allows you
to build a vision of where you want to get to and map
out how to get there. Hope is a good starting point,
but it's not enough—channel your sisu
to plan, strategize, and act.

Family Journey

In late 2011, Marko Albrecht set out to make a simple film for his newborn twins, piecing together footage from old family videos and photos to show them how the sisu mind-set shaped his life. The project evolved into an emotional five-year journey for Albrecht and his extended family after his uncle Heikki was diagnosed with terminal cancer. In the resulting award-winning documentary, *Sisu: Family, Perseverance and Love from Finland to America,* family members reflect on what sisu means to them. "Never surrendering," "persevering no matter how many times life knocks you down," "having the guts and balls to get through the most difficult of times and still survive," they said. Uncle Heikki concluded: "Sisu is bravery, perseverance, and the will to do things right."

Calm in a Storm

One trait associated with sisu is stoicism.
This can be invaluable at times of intense adversity,
helping you to retain a rational, objective perspective
when swirling emotions could easily cloud your better
judgment. While others around you are losing their heads,
you may need to find a quiet corner and withdraw into
yourself despite the pressure of the situation. Such a
response could be mistaken for stolid indifference, but
if it allows you to channel your inner sisu toward
finding a solution and leads to bold action,
people will soon come to understand.

66 If you can learn
to embrace the tide
of adversity, you will
eventually learn to
let it lift you up and
you can ride the wave
to shore, unscathed. **99**

———

Marcus Aurelius Anderson,
mind-set coach

Stubbornness

People with a strong sense of sisu are liable to exhibit an element of stubbornness. You need it to keep pushing ahead when the naysayers are saying nay. However, stubbornness can be unproductive if it manifests itself in pig-headed intransigence and in the refusal to look at alternative options, back down in an argument, or admit mistakes. If you are impossible to communicate with, you might be alienating someone who could help. When applied correctly, sisu is about pursuing a righteous path with determination, imagination, and patience. Aspire to stubbornness that makes you lean into an issue and explore all avenues to resolve it while remaining considerate to others.

Through the Mist

Anyone who has suffered a serious bout
of depression will attest to the feeling of utter
helplessness when in its grip—the crippling perception
that there is no way forward and nothing will ever be
better again. Getting out of bed, doing housework,
socializing with people . . . doing anything seems like
a monumental effort under the weight of your woes.
At such extreme times of crisis, tapping into your
sisu can encourage you to see through the mist,
seek the help you need, and begin the process
of recovery one small step at a time.

Get Up, Don't Give Up

———

Finland has produced some of the greatest
endurance athletes of all time, and four-time Olympic
gold medalist Lasse Virén is right up there. Virén had a
bigger heart than the average man (literally) and pushed
his limits with more than 750 training sessions per year,
many during the cruel Finnish winter. But it was in the
1972 Olympic 10,000-meter final that he had to delve
deepest into his sisu power reserves. After suffering a fall
halfway through the race, he fought back and not only won
the race, but set a new world-record time. So when life trips
you up, make like Lasse: Get up, remain concentrated on
your goal, and give it all you've got to get there.

" The secret of Lasse Virén can be found in his rigid persistence . . . Lasse was able to find unbelievable strength. He could stretch his limits like a rubber band. **"**

Rolf Haikkola, coach of legendary athlete Lasse Virén

3

SEEKING SOLUTIONS

Finns have a hard-earned reputation as expert problem-solvers. Learn how to leverage your latent sisu strength to push through challenges and achieve transformative change.

PRAGMATISM

———

While sisu is about envisioning a better future
and actively taking steps to realize that vision in even
the most trying of circumstances, a sense of the past can
helpfully inform your endeavors. Acceptance that such
targets are rarely, if ever, achieved smoothly will cushion
the blow of inevitable disappointments along the way,
especially when setting grander aims. With the real-world
pragmatism inherent in sisu, such setbacks strengthen,
rather than diminish, your resolve.

Break It Down

———

Aim high, but be realistic about the journey
to the summit of your ambitions. Make a level-headed
assessment of where you are and where you want to get to.
Identify the factors under your control and take action to
deal with them and tip the odds in your favor. Even if your
intended target seems distant, don't allow yourself to
be daunted. Break the task down into manageable
chunks—what you can you do today, tomorrow, and
the next day—and let your inner sisu direct you.

Agility

With sisu, you can tackle seemingly insuperable
problems with the panache of a parkour practitioner
traversing the urban jungle. The traceur visualizes his or
her route then sets off with total conviction. Vaulting over
walls, tiptoeing along slim ledges, grabbing onto railings,
and leaping seemingly impossible distances from roof
to roof. Spinning, tumbling, swinging, backflipping,
somersaulting, rolling, crawling . . . whatever it takes to
conquer the obstructions in the way. You, too, can learn
to be alert to the unexpected and to relax sufficiently to
cushion the impact when landing a big jump, before
pushing on fearlessly to attack the next obstacle.

Resourcefulness

———

Make the most of what you've got. See how Finland has
become a leading light in the global technology sector.
You might expect to find cutting-edge equipment in
all classrooms to train the tech heads of tomorrow.
Instead pupils often learn using outdated, but perfectly
serviceable computers. Without distraction from shiny, new
features, children are able to build a foundation of essential
knowledge, extract the most they can from the available
equipment, and develop their creativity. Then, when
they get to use the latest tech, they are ready to fly.
Limitations can breed limitless creativity.

THINK DIFFERENTLY

—

For people who tend to be low-key and understated in
their general manner, Finns often stand out from the crowd
as pioneers through their actions. Indeed, the ingenuity and
experimental attitude inherent in sisu can lead you down
unexpected avenues. But if sisu is guiding you, why not go
against the grain? Don't let the fear of embarrassment or
criticism for doing things differently deter you from
exploring. A problem you've never encountered before
may require blue-sky thinking to solve it.

" Every great and deep difficulty bears in itself its own solution. It forces us to change our thinking in order to find it. "

———

Niels Bohr, physicist

Whatever Works

Finns are never shy about adopting successful
methods from other parts of the world if they
feel they will work in their own country. Take the
country's much-lauded universal healthcare system.
When it was reformed after World War II, Finland
leaned heavily on contemporary British and American
blueprints. There is nothing wrong with drawing on
proven ideas and then taking them forward, adapting
them to the particular circumstances you, your
family, or community as a whole may face.
Whatever works is good.

Lengthen Your Stride

The slippery concept of "talent" is not conducive to personal development. How often do you read about "gifted" people as if they are imbued with magical powers beyond the reach of other mortals? If you believe you lack the talent to achieve, you are defeated. So never think of your ability as fixed. Sisu gives you the courage and can-do attitude to learn the skills needed. Learn from the legendary Finnish athlete of the early-twentieth century Paavo Nurmi, who used to run holding onto the buffer of a train in order to lengthen his stride, and see how you can extend your range of competence. And when you achieve what once seemed impossible, you will surely wonder what else you can do.

Attention

Outsiders often marvel at Finland's high child-literacy
rates and wonder how they are achieved when kids
only begin formal reading instruction at age seven.
American researcher Martha Brueggeman went into
schools in Helsinki and in the town of Hämeenlinna to
search for the secrets. She observed young children
listening attentively to teachers reading stories,
determined to understand. They completed schoolwork
independently and quietly. And those same students
sang and danced animatedly to folk songs in assembly.
The common thread, Brueggeman observed, was sisu,
which helped the kids give their full attention to each
task. "Sisu is found in the classroom," she said.

Dare to Fail

———

The fear of failure can be paralyzing, but if you don't try, you will never know. That's why, in 2010, a group of Finnish university students inaugurated a Day for Failure in recognition that mishaps are inevitable en route to success. Since then, many prominent businessmen, sportspeople, artists, politicians, and other high achievers have shared stories of their failings to inspire others to try new things without fear of the consequences. But why wait until the official Day for Failure on October 13 each year? Fortified by sisu, every day can be a failure day if it means you tried something ambitious! Don't see failed attempts as an ultimate failure. Get back on the horse and try again.

66 The journey of
a thousand miles
begins with a
single step. **99**

———

Laozi, ancient Chinese philosopher

Productive Postmortems

———

Many "positive-thinkers" refuse to review their failures, preferring to bury the memory and simply look to the future. What are they scared of? Is their confidence so shallow that they cannot face the truth of their faults for fear of mental disintegration? With a sisu state of mind, you can learn to relish a thorough postmortem on an unsuccessful initiative. Rather than perceive such missteps as irredeemable calamities, take them as opportunities to learn and grow stronger. Constructive analysis ultimately yields progress, because next time you will be more alert to the pitfalls. The only way to learn is to try, test, adapt, and evolve.

4

STRONGER
TOGETHER

Sisu makes each of us more self-sufficient,
but its power increases exponentially when
people collaborate to work for the common good.

Self-made?

The idea that anyone is completely "self-made" is a myth. Success is never achieved alone. No matter how self-sufficient you might think you are, each day you benefit from the efforts of others. The bed you sleep in, the clothes you wear, the roads you travel, the places you visit, the food you eat . . . every aspect is built upon the multifarious contributions of your fellow citizens, cooperating as innovators, designers, laborers, producers, and more. Your life is supported by thousands of people you may never meet, so it is only logical to use your sisu to enhance your own contribution to society as a whole.

Priorities

People are capable of the extraordinary; it is just a matter of channeling that ability toward the priorities first. In Finland, it is widely understood that individuals cannot have freedom without the firm foundation of solid, cooperative communities, public services that benefit all, and safe streets. Ensuring that these basic needs are met first leaves people freer of worries that they won't be able to deal financially with unexpected events, and to push forward and pursue their individual goals. A high degree of self-sufficiency is expected in Finland, and sisu gives its citizens the strength to cope with all manner of problems, but it has also helped to create a safety net for when they can't.

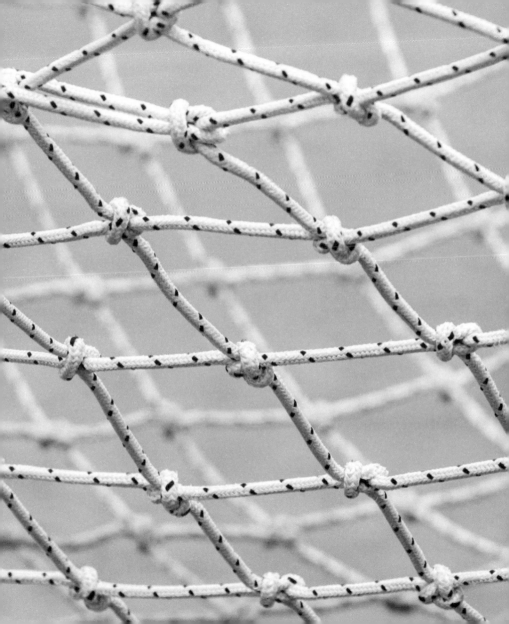

STRIPS OF
INGENUITY

—

A 1996 survey of Finnish Americans by Eleanor Palo Stoller offered an anecdotal snapshot of the extent to which their ancestors back home went to pay huge reparations to the Soviet Union after World War II. "My mother had a tablecloth made out of little strips of paper," recalled one respondent. "They used paper tablecloths so they could sell their fabric abroad, keep their freedom, and not be one of the Russian satellites." This serves as a fine example of sisu, sacrifice, and ingenuity to address a national priority.

One for All

———

Sisu scholar Emilia Lahti uses her own action mind-set to spread awareness of the concept. She believes that, by fostering sisu as individuals, our reprogramed behavior can influence whole communities. In 2018, she ran the entire length of New Zealand in fifty days. The challenge was branded "Sisu not Silence." A survivor of domestic violence, Lahti aimed to make the issue more prevalent in public discourse, remove the stigma imposed on individuals who have experienced it, and set a positive example for fellow "overcomers." The event marked an individual pursuit for a communal cause, fueled by an epic amount of sisu.

Reach Out

A sisu mind-set fosters a high level of self-sufficiency,
but sometimes the stress upon you goes beyond the point
at which you can just stiffen your upper lip and battle
on alone. One of the negative manifestations of sisu is
when extreme pride precludes asking others for help.
Remember, it also takes sisu to have the courage to
open up, to share personal problems, and to acknowledge
our human frailties. A trusted friend, work colleague,
or family member will want to help. With sisu, one
thing is for sure—inaction is not an option.

THINK INSIDE
THE (BABY) BOX

———

The "Baby Box" given by the state to all expectant mothers in Finland exemplifies how sisu can be applied to important communal issues. The box contains fifty-odd essential items, including reusable diapers, all types of clothing, bathing products, and a mattress—the box itself can even be used as a cot. This starter kit for life was introduced in the 1930s as part of a package of measures to help reduce the country's high infant-mortality rate. It was a difficult problem and an expensive undertaking for what was a poor country. Today, Finland has one of world's lowest rates of both maternal and infant death, and newborn children begin life's journey on a more even footing.

Talkoohenki

For first-generation Finnish immigrants to the
United States, helping each other was a matter of survival.
This spirit of cooperation, or *talkoohenki*, bolstered by sisu,
enabled people to build vital facilities, fight for better
working conditions, and pool resources during hard times.
The tradition of *talkoot* events continues in Finland,
with volunteers pitching in to do jobs in the local area
for the communal good. So, if you see jobs that need doing
in your neighborhood, summon up the spirit of
those Finnish pioneers, organize your own *talkoot*,
and take collective action. Your reward? A better
environment and the respect of your peers.

66 Finns are faring so well because we have a different mindset [*sic*] about success—one that's based on equity and community. 99

———

Jorma Ollila, former CEO of Nokia

Straight Talk

———

Finns may not be renowned as extravagant
conversationalists, but they have proven to be erudite
and highly effective communicators. When you speak
with a Finn, you are unlikely to be left in any doubt of his
or her opinion. If everyone is encouraged to be similarly
straightforward, difficult issues are confronted head on and
resolution may be found more quickly. The more a group
takes on this mode of communication, the less people will
become offended by differences of opinion. And everyone
will benefit from the best proposals being shared.

War and Peace

—

The world woke up to the potency of Finnish sisu in battle during the Winter War, but the persistence and solution-oriented thinking engendered by sisu can equally be applied to conflict resolution. Former Finland president Martti Ahtisaari was awarded the Nobel Peace Prize in 2008 in recognition of his three decades as an international peace mediator. Ahtisaari's early childhood experience of his hometown of Viborg being annexed by the Soviet Union during the Winter War influenced his choice of work and his no-nonsense style of diplomacy got results in places ranging from Namibia to Indonesia. "You have to be rather straightforward with your clients," he said. "You can't tell the parties only nice things. This is not an entertainment show."

Enjoy the Silence

Visitors to Finland will soon discover that its inhabitants are very comfortable with silence. For the perennial chatterers among us, such long pauses in conversation can by unnerving. But be brave. Mindless talk can distract from addressing the real issues. And the gaps may be more meaningful than anything you have to say in that moment. So relish the silence and the space to gather your thoughts. Then when you have something significant to contribute, your words will carry more weight.

66 The fewer the words,
the better the prayer. **99**

Martin Luther, theologian

RESPECT

Always speak your mind, but give time and space for
the other person(s) to share their perspective . . . and listen
to it, consider it. Stand your ground if you totally disagree.
But perhaps there is some room for constructive compromise
to find an even better way forward. If these principles
are universally observed, everyone will feel they have
been heard and respected, and no one will be
inhibited from expressing an opinion.

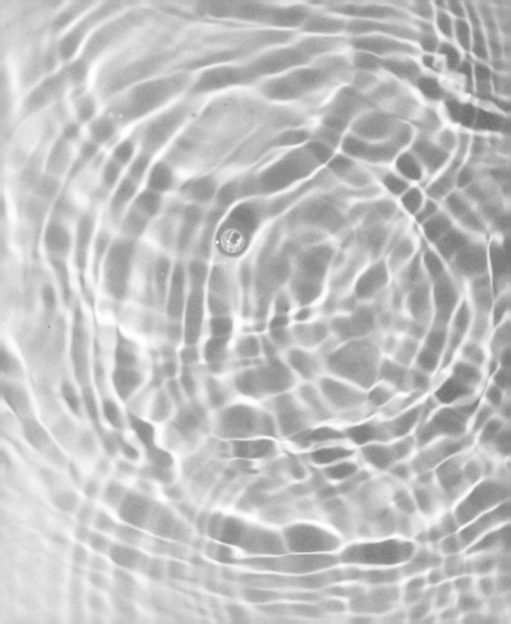

Self-deprecation

We are all just tiny specks in the vastness of the universe. Everything we do causes ripples, sometimes waves, but no matter how significant our accomplishments, they pale in comparison to the accumulated achievements of billions of other people on the planet and the generations that came before us. This reality is perhaps why Finns are more liable to talk themselves down than up, even though Finland punches well above its weight for a relatively small nation. Being self-effacing, rather than overbearing, removes the chance of those around us feeling belittled or unworthy. And, with sisu, we know we can rise to the occasion when needed, so why shout about it?

Keep Your Promises

———

With a sisu mind-set, you will expand your abilities
and consequently expect more from yourself. But if you are
honest with yourself, it will prevent you from making rash
pledges. Finns take promises seriously and so should you.
It's better to manage expectations and then overachieve
than lose the confidence of your peers by falling short
of hopelessly optimistic claims. If you promise to do
something, do everything in your power to make it happen.
Don't give up at the first sign of difficulty. And never resort
to lying and cheating; dishonesty is a lazy shortcut that
doesn't fit with the sisu imperative of confronting life's
conundrums. Act with integrity, be true to your word,
and it will encourage others to follow suit.

5

NURTURING
SISU

Let's explore proactive ways to
develop sisu and expand our capacities
to manage the vagaries of life.

Mind and Body

———

There is a symbiotic relationship between the sisu mind-set and your physical and mental well-being. Sisu can help you to push beyond your normal physical capabilities out of necessity and in the face of adversity. Doing so increases your strength, resilience, and endurance. Additionally, if you take care of your well-being—through eating well, regular exercise, and restorative breaks in nature—you will nourish your sisu and feel better equipped to cope with the vicissitudes of fortune.

TEST OR REGRESS

———

"It's tough to get out of bed to do roadwork at 5 a.m. when you've been sleeping in silk pajamas." So said boxing champion Marvelous Marvin Hagler on his retirement from the sport. And it is true that, when we reach a level of comfort, it is easy to lose some of the tenacity that earned us our luxuries. But the sisu construct is a recognition that human beings need to experience challenges to feel fully alive and thrive. If we never test ourselves, we gradually regress. Sure, take time to enjoy the fruits of your toil, but when one demanding chapter of your life closes, look out for new ways to exercise your sisu muscle.

Parental Guidance

Here are some ideas to proactively help your children plug into their sisu power source: Instill in them a love of learning; encourage effort and perseverance, rather than give out unmerited gold stars; help them to see failures as bumps in the road to discovery, not reasons to give up; allow them to learn the satisfaction of reaching goals they've worked hard to achieve; embolden them to be independent, self-reliant, and take on responsibility, but also encourage them to have the courage to ask for help; endow them with the knowledge that they are one of many and show them how communal efforts can achieve extraordinary things; encourage outdoor activities in all conditions to develop resilience; and just let kids be kids, with plenty of unstructured time for them to explore, experience life, and discover their passions.

Live to Learn, Learn to Live

It is fitting that the world's most literate nation chose to celebrate the centenary of its independence by building a state-of-the-art public library. The Helsinki Central Library Oodi, opened in December 2018, stands opposite the Parliament House as a symbol of Finland's continuing commitment to the lifelong learning and active citizenship that has been so vital to the country's development. While libraries worldwide face budget cuts, Finland invested millions on Library Oodi, reimagining the traditional template to attract new generations with everything from an audio-visual recording studio to a "makerspace" with 3-D printers. You may not have such a facility within reach, but in a fast-changing, challenging world, maintaining a determination to learn and adapt is a necessity. Draw on your sisu and commit to a life of endless discovery.

" Curiosity is, in great
and generous minds,
the first passion
and the last. **"**

———

Samuel Johnson, author

UNPLUG AND RECONNECT

It is so easy to get distracted in the modern world. Our smartphones are mobile entertainment centers with music, games, photos, messaging services, all available at the swipe of a screen. Social media offers a 24/7 feed of friends' latest activities and breaking news you probably don't need to know right now. If you're not careful, you'll lose track of who you are and what most needs attention in your life. Instead, take time out each day to reconnect with yourself and refocus. Put down the tablet, take off the headphones, and get outside. Look up at the sky, follow the movement of the clouds, listen to the birds, and the breeze rustling through the trees. The answers are whispering in the waiting room of your subconscious if you'll only stop to listen.

Working Holiday

––––––––––

Although the vast majority of Finnish people are now
urbanites, the nation's rural roots are still infused into
public consciousness, and many Finns love to escape to the
wilderness. When summer finally comes, a popular vacation
is to retreat to a small cabin, or *mökki*, in a forest, by a lake,
or in the middle of nowhere for a good four weeks. It is
likely to be more basic than the family home, perhaps
lacking central heating, electricity, or running water, but for
mökki diehards chopping firewood, collecting water, and
generally being self-sufficient is part of the pleasure.
If you need a sisu-rejuvenating break, maybe choose the
mökkielämä (cabin lifestyle) over all-inclusive luxury.

Take the Plunge

Winter swimming in the sea or one of its 188,000-odd
lakes is popular in Finland. This leisure activity is sisu
in a microcosm. First, there's the willpower it takes to lower
yourself into frigid waters, followed by the resolution to
deal with the initial shock without jumping straight back
out again. But, oh, the reward as your body adjusts to the
chill—an invigorating surge of feel-good hormones and a
reinforced connection to nature. A regular dip, even for just
half a minute, has health benefits galore—from relieving
stress, aches, and pains to burning calories and boosting the
immune system. If you have the chance (and only after
taking medical advice), seek out a winter swimming club,
summon up your sisu, and take the plunge!

Chill Out at Home

———

If you don't have easy access to a frozen lake
(or the Baltic Sea) but want to reap some of the
benefits of winter swimming, a good substitute is taking
a cold shower. To get some cold hydrotherapy at home,
simply turn on the cold faucet for a few seconds at the end
of your shower to make your body tingle and jolt
yourself into action. As your tolerance grows, extend
your time spent under the chilling spray.

Feel the Heat

———

For winter swimmers, combining a soothing sauna session with a dip in ice-cold water is the ultimate reinvigorator. It was once written that if you want to experience heaven and hell simultaneously, go to a Finnish sauna, and if you can take the heat, the benefits are manifold. As water is ladled over the birch twigs and hot stones, revel in the aroma and feel the tension and fatigue melt away as the temperature rises. Whether you go there for peaceful contemplation or to talk through issues with friends, the sauna is a wonderful place to reflect, reset, revive, and get ready for your next challenge.

PEAK SISU

Who better to turn to for advice on constructing a sisu mind-set than Veikka Gustafsson, the first Finn ever to climb Everest. This national sisu icon even named his son Sisu. In an interview a quarter of a century after his 1993 Everest expedition—by which time he'd scaled all of the world's tallest mountains—Gustafsson revealed some of his tried-and-tested strategies: "Stick with your decisions no matter what," "Think of how earlier generations coped with the difficulties you face," "If you are uncomfortable treat it as an experience," and "Remember that the biggest obstacles are between our ears, what we tell ourselves."

Everyday Sisu

———

Small acts of sisu in everyday life incubate
an action mind-set. Have that difficult conversation
you've been putting off. Put in the extra effort to make
a healthy meal from scratch rather than order takeout.
Launch that community project you've been pondering.
Sign up for the training course you've been considering.
Persist with a half-finished DIY job that had you stumped.
Start writing that novel. And remember: If you can make
a habit of doing the thing you need to do most on
waking each day—even if it's the thing you least
want to do—the rest of the day will be downhill.

" You can slowly but surely implement sisu into your way of thinking so that it's second nature to persevere through the most difficult, arduous situations. **"**

Heikki Väänänen, CEO and founder
of HappyOrNot

Take Care

———

Work diligently until your body aches and your
brain hurts and earn the pleasure of a deep, restful sleep,
safe in knowledge that your efforts have taken you closer
to realizing your ambitions. The Finns have shown that a
Lutheran work ethic and sisu sensibility offers valuable
dividends. But beware of pushing too hard for too long or
burnout beckons. Applying sisu to work to the long-term
detriment of your health and personal relationships is a
misuse of this precious inner resource. Remain vigilant and
withdraw from the fray when you need time to recuperate.

Build Character

In this era of social media and vacuous celebrity culture, there is an emphasis on projecting an idealized version of life. Witness the millions of pouting selfies posted each day, the not-so-humble brags, and elaborate attempts to grab the limelight amid the global cacophony of noise. We've learned how Finns value achievement over attention-seeking antics, substance over the superficial. So get real. Stop trying to present a personality and dig deep to develop true character. Learn new skills to shape the world around you for the better. Stand up for your beliefs and for those less fortunate. Orienting your sisu toward building a life of integrity will ultimately be far more rewarding than a few retweets.

MOBILIZE

—

Resilience is not built by sitting around. If that sounds
like you, look for ways to move more. You don't necessarily
need to join a gym or a sports team to get a workout
if that's not your scene; there are many simple ways you can
make exercise an incidental part of your day. See household
chores as a chance to stretch and lift. Take the stairs instead
of the elevator. Walk, run, or cycle some or all of your way
to work. Jog around the park with the toddler in a pram.
And get outside whatever the weather. Get practical outdoor
clothing, and you can face the elements and feed off
their energy any day. No excuses.

" [Sisu] means you don't see a silver lining, but you jump into the storm anyway. There is something that elicits hope in sisu. **"**

———

Emilia Lahti, researcher, public speaker, and social activist

Go Big

We have seen how Finland has boldly overcome some of
the biggest challenges imaginable, from its battles for
independence to transforming its education, health, and
welfare systems to improve the lives of all its inhabitants.
So when you see a problem that needs to be fixed, no matter
how daunting its scale, go all-in, no half measures. The pace
of progress may be slow at times and the roadmap to your
goal may seem impossibly complicated, but with the spirit
of sisu you will explore all avenues to get there.

Spread the Word

———

Now you have a word to describe this awesome
psychological potential inside us all, talk to others about
sisu. Imagine the transformational power of social groups,
communities, towns, and cities all sharing a sisu state of
mind. Imagine the multiplier effects if everyone practiced
sisu, each becoming more willing to act boldly and
cooperate for the common good; more resilient, motivated,
and determined to persevere in the face of adversity.

But you don't need to imagine—just look at the
disproportionate successes of the small nation of Finland.
Take steps to harness your personal sisu, lead by
example, and pass the message on.

Resources

Books

Karjalainen, Jesse. *Sisu: Resilience Belonging Purpose—The Secrets of Finland's Can-do Mindset*. Amazon Kindle.

Nylund, Joanna. *Sisu: The Finnish Art of Courage*. London: Octopus, 2018.

Pantzar, Katja. *Finding Sisu: In Search of Courage, Strength, and Happiness the Finnish Way*. London: Hodder & Stoughton, 2018.

Tokoi, Oskari. *Sisu: Even Through a Stone Wall: The Autobiography of Oskari Tokoi*. New York: Robert Speller & Sons, Publishers, Inc., 1957.

Journal articles

Brueggeman, Martha A. "An Outsider's View of Beginning Literacy in Finland: Assumptions, Lessons Learned, and Sisu." *Literacy Research and Instruction*, Vol. 47; No. 1, 2007.

Haikkola, Rolf. "The Secret of Sisu and the Making of Lasse Virén." *Track and Field News*, Pt. 198, 2012.

Lahti, Emilia. "Embodied Fortitude: An Introduction to the Finnish Construct of Sisu." *International Journal of Wellbeing*, Vol. 9; No.1.

Palo Stoller, Eleanor. "Sauna, Sisu, and Sibelius: Ethnic Identity Among Finnish Americans." *Sociological Quarterly*, Vol. 37; No. 1, 1996.

Sinkkonen, Jari. "The Land of Sauna, Sisu, and Sibelius—An Attempt at a Psychological Portrait of Finland." *International Journal of Applied Psychoanalytic Studies*, Vol. 10; No. 1, March, 2013.

Taramaa, Raija. "Stubborn and Silent Finns with 'Sisu' in Finnish-American Literature: An Imagological Study of Finnishness in the Literary Production of Finnish-American Authors." Oulu: Oulun yliopisto, 2007.

Online articles

Baer, Drake. "This Untranslatable Finnish Word Takes Perseverance to a Whole New Level." businessinsider.com, June 17, 2014.

Bonasera, Carina. "The World's Happiest Country Uses the Concept 'Sisu'; Here's Why You Should Too." thriveglobal.com, April 15, 2019.

Ollila, Jorma. "Why Finland Comes out on Top on Happiness and More." latimes.com, April 7, 2019.

Smirnova, Olga. "Sisu: The Finnish Art of Inner Strength." bbc.com, May 7, 2018.

Spector, Nicole. "What the World's Happiest Country can Teach Americans." nbcnews.com, March 24, 2019.

Väänänen, Heikki. "Why Business Leaders Should Follow 'Sisu,' Finland's Equivalent Of The American Dream." forbes.com, March 6, 2019.

Online resources

Anderson, Marcus Aurelius. "The Gift of Adversity." TEDx Talk via youtube.com, May 31, 2017.

emilialahti.com

Lahti, Emilia. "Sisu—Transforming Barriers into Frontiers." TEDx Talk via youtube.com, December 15, 2014.

sisufilm.org

sisulab.com

Picture Credits

2, 10, 32, 58, 84, 116 Shutterstock/krrowl48; 5, 97 Shutterstock/solarbird; 7 Shutterstock/ namtipStudio; 8 Shutterstock/Jarhe Photography; 12 Shutterstock/Pavel_Klimenko; 13 Shutterstock/ SasaStock; 15, 87, 152–153, 156–157 Shutterstock/Ville heikkinen; 17 Shutterstock/sirtravelalot; 18 Shutterstock/Kichigin; 19 Shutterstock/cristovao; 21 Shutterstock/oroch; 23 Shutterstock/Donald R. Swartz; 24: Wikimedia Commons/CC-BY-SA-4.0; 27 Shutterstock/Lukas Gojda; 28 Shutterstock/ Petri jauhiainen; 29 Shutterstock/Denis Belitsky; 30 Shutterstock/wacomka; 35 Shutterstock/ NancyP5; 37 Shutterstock/ArCaLu; 38–39 Shutterstock/Dziewul; 41 Shutterstock/Krzysztof_ Jankowski; 42 Shutterstock/Alexander Erdbeer; 43 Shutterstock/Tom Grundy; 45 Shutterstock/ FREEDOMPIC; 46 Shutterstock/Petri Volanen; 47 Shutterstock/Edward Fielding; 49 Shutterstock/ Sandra Huber; 50 Shutterstock/Rico van Winkel; 51 Shutterstock/Roman Babakin; 52 Shutterstock/ Lari Saukkonen. 55, 75 Shutterstock/Suzanne Tucker; 57; Shutterstock/Hitdelight; 61 Shutterstock/ Aleksey Stemmer; 63 Shutterstock/Alex Staroseltsev; 64 Shutterstock/haraldmuc; 65 Shutterstock/ Arsenii Palivoda; 67 Shutterstock/Pressmaster; 68 Shutterstock/Aleksey Stemmer; 69 Shutterstock/ Opasbbb; 71 Shutterstock/erdalislakphotography; 72 Shutterstock/Zolnierek; 76–77 Shutterstock/ Thomas Bethge; 78 Shutterstock/Marcel Poncu; 79 Shutterstock/Svetlana.Is; 81 Shutterstock/ Mumemories; 83 Shutterstock/AndreyUG; 86 Shutterstock/Milosz_G; 89 Shutterstock/Kerdkanno; 90 Shutterstock/Andrey_Kuzmin; 91 Shutterstock/Quang Ho; 92 Shutterstock/Photosebia; 95 Shutterstock/Freedom Studio; 96 Shutterstock/Tatyana Vyc; 99 Shutterstock/Wollertz; 101 Shutterstock/Richard Cavalleri; 102 Shutterstock/dotshock; 105 Shutterstock/Kostenko Maxim; 107 Shutterstock/Jani Riekkinen; 109 Shutterstock/Jarmo Piironen; 110 Shutterstock/Song_about_ summer; 111 Shutterstock/nadtytok; 112–113 Shutterstock/leungchopan; 105 Shutterstock/file404; 119 Shutterstock/Dmytro Flisak; 120 Shutterstock/stocksolutions; 121 Shutterstock/Sandra Cunningham, 122 Shutterstock/Bildagentur Zoonar GmbH; 125 Shutterstock/watermelonart; 127 Shutterstock/Erik Mandre; 128 Shutterstock/Ingrid Maasik; 129 Shutterstock/sirastock; 130 Shutterstock/Ekaterina Kondratova; 131 Shutterstock/Baranova Anna; 133 Shutterstock/Andras Pal; 135 Shutterstock/Mark Sayer; 136 Shutterstock/Lana Kray;138 Shutterstock/Daniel Prudek; 139 Shutterstock/wacomka; 141 Shutterstock/aboikis; 142 Shutterstock/SariMe; 143 Shutterstock/ yari2000; 147 Shutterstock/symbiot; 148 Shutterstock/Poznyakov; 149 Shutterstock/gorillaimages; 151 Shutterstock/Pictureguy; 155 Shutterstock/VGstockstudio.